THE ACA LEGAL SERIES

Volume 9

"THIRD-PARTY PAYMENTS"

THE ACA LEGAL SERIES:

Series Editor: Theodore P. Remley, Jr., JD, Ph.D.

THE ACA LEGAL SERIES

Volume 9

"THIRD-PARTY PAYMENTS"

J. Steve Strosnider, MA
John D. Grad, JD

Series Editor
Theodore P. Remley, Jr., JD, PhD

American Counseling Association
5999 Stevenson Avenue
Alexandria, VA 22304

Cover Design by Sarah Jane Valdez

Library of Congress Cataloging-in-Publication Data

Strosnider, J. Steve.
  Third party payments/J. Steve Strosnider, John D. Grad.
  p.   cm. — (The ACA legal series; v.9)
  Includes bibliographical references.
  ISBN 1-55620-124-9
  1. Insurance, Health—Law and legislation—United States. 2. Third
parties (Law)—United States. I. Grad, John D. II. Title. III. Series.
KF1183.S77   1993
346.73'086382—dc20
[347.30686382]
                                                        93-13262
                                                        CIP

Printed in the United States of America

Contents

14177

Biographies

J. Steve Strosnider is a licensed professional counselor and director of the Department of Counseling and Psychology at Lewis-Gale Clinic in Salem, Virginia. He has served in a variety of clinical and administrative settings. He is currently a member of the Virginia Board of Professional Counselors and past president of the Virginia Association of Clinical Counselors. He holds a BS degree in psychology from Virginia Commonwealth University in Richmond and an MA degree in clinical psychology from Appalachian State University in Boone, North Carolina, and he has had additional graduate training in counseling, group psychotherapy, and family studies at the College of William and Mary, Eastern Virginia Medical School, and Virginia Tech. He is certified by the National Board for Certified Counselors and the National Academy of Certified Clinical Mental Health Counselors.

Mr. Strosnider has been active in legislative affairs dealing with health insurance reimbursement for professional counselors as well as with mental health consumer issues. He is the author of several publications and articles dealing with a variety of counseling subjects.

John D. Grad practices law in the areas of civil rights, health, and litigation. He represents numerous physicians in matters of licensure, ethics, insurance reimbursement, malpractice, hospital privileges, Medicare enforcement matters, and other topics. Mr. Grad graduated Phi Beta Kappa from Hamilton College and from the New York University School of Law, where he was a Root-Tilden Scholar. Currently, Mr. Grad is a partner in the Alexandria, Virginia, law firm of Grad, Logan, & Klewans, PC. He is a member of the Virginia State Bar, the District of Columbia Bar, and the New York State Bar.

Mr. Grad is a member of many professional societies, including the National Health Lawyers and the Foundation of the Alexandria Bar Association, of which he has been president since 1989. He is a past president of the Alexandria Bar Association and is currently a member of the Virginia Bar Council, the governing body of the Virginia Bar. He is also member of the ethics faculty of the Virginia Bar, the governing board of the Virginia Bar Health Law Section, the Virginia Bar Committee on Lawyer Advertising, and he was formerly on the board of the American Society of Law and Medicine.

Theodore P. Remley, Jr., Series Editor, is Executive Director of the American Counseling Association. Immediately prior to assuming this position, Dr. Remley was chair of the Department of Counselor Education at Mississippi State University in Starkville. He holds a PhD from the Department of Counselor Education at the University of Florida in Gainesville and a JD in law from the Catholic University of America in Washington, DC.

Preface

The authors, a professional counselor and an attorney dealing with the health profession, have observed the struggles of professional counselors to achieve recognition as practitioners eligible for third-party reimbursements by health insurance carriers. Although professional counselors deserve this recognition, in our experience most counselors are not yet prepared to understand and comply with federal, state, and insurance company regulations. These regulations often involve subtle nuances yet are also subject to rapid and dramatic changes.

Becoming informed about the subject, however, can be vital to professional livelihood. A recent survey revealed that approximately 60% of the clients of mental health practitioners in private practice possessed third-party coverage. The percentage of therapists' income paid by insurance was approximately 47%. At the same time, therapists reported more trouble than ever in obtaining reimbursement by insurance companies, with approximately 45% feeling that the situation was "getting worse" ("Fee and Practice," 1992).

These numbers merely evidence what the authors and many in the field believe: Professional counselors are often uninformed about insurance matters, which in turn is a part of the problem for the profession in achieving proper reimbursement status. Other parts of the problem are the changes in health care reimbursement that can occur quite rapidly, the licensing requirements for counselors that vary from state to state, and the lack of uniform standards as well as legislative differences in terms of the scope of practices.

In addition, laws vary from state to state in terms of counselors and recognition by third-party payers. For example, professional counselors are licensed in 35 states, but reimbursement is only mandated by statute in 10 states (Blue Cross/Blue Shield Association, 1992). Another factor that needs to be considered is the rapid proliferation of managed care, preferred provider organizations (PPOs), and health maintenance organizations (HMOs).

This monograph is intended as a guide for counselors on participating in third-party reimbursement activities in an effective and legal manner. The particulars, the specifics, are sure to change; but the issues and general concepts related to the third-party reimbursement presented here in broad outlines should remain useful over time.

Thus this monograph introduces the world of third-party reimbursers and addresses general issues related to professional counselors and health care reimbursement. It describes major health reimbursement plans such as Blue Cross, Blue Shield, CHAMPUS, and Medicaid/Medicare as well as self-insured plans and private health insurance companies. Federal regulations, which often supersede state statutes, and such concepts as extraterritoriality and freedom of choice, which vary from state to state, are introduced. General concepts related to the legal requirements for health care reimbursement as well as strategies for maximizing reimbursement are also discussed. Readers should note that the information provided is as accurate as possible at this time, but that federal, state, and insurance company regulations inevitably change.

Legal issues are only broadly discussed in this monograph. Nothing in this publication should be construed as legal advice. The information here is intended to serve as guidelines and to be educational regarding general issues. Mental health professionals should consult with their individual attorneys regarding specific legal problems; and readers with questions about specific coverages should consult specific employers, state or federal agencies, professional organizations, or insurance carriers.

Glossary

Administrator: A company that handles the paperwork and the transfer of funds for an employer who has a self-insured plan.

Assignment of Benefits: Authorization of the client for the third-party reimburser to compensate the provider directly.

Beneficiary: The individual, not necessarily the client, who is eligible for benefits under insurance contracts, synonymous with *the insured.*

Benefit Period: A period of time, usually 12 months, after which new deductibles must accumulate before benefits will be paid, and limited yearly benefits exceeded are not reimbursed.

Carrier: The insurance company or entity responsible for the processing and administration of claims.

Civilian Health and Medical Program of the Uniformed Services (CHAMPUS): The health benefit program for families of U.S. military personnel, including retired personnel.

Claim: A request for payment from an insurance carrier.

COBRA (Consolidated Omnibus Budget Reconciliation Act): The legislation that provides for continued insurance coverage for a limited time to employees who have lost health insurance benefits because they were terminated or their work hours were reduced.

Coordination of Benefits: The arrangements by which two or more insurance carriers reimburse for services rendered, avoiding payments for more than the actual fee charged.

CPT-4 (Physicians Current Procedural Terminology): The American Medical Association (1991) publication for physicians that lists terms and identifies codes for reporting medical services.

Copayment: The dollar amount paid by the client rather than the third party.

Counselor: A person who provides professional counseling services that may be reimbursable under health insurance policies. In some states, mental health practitioners must be licensed to practice.

Covered Services: Services eligible for reimbursement as defined by an insurance contract.

Deductible: A specific dollar amount the insured must pay, typically at the beginning of each benefit or insurance contract year, before reimbursement begins. There are individual deductibles (e.g., $250) and family deductibles (e.g., $500) that must be met before benefits begin.

Diagnostic and Statistical Manual of Mental Disorders, 3rd Edition, Revised (DSM-III-R): The American Psychiatric Association (1987) publication that lists diagnostic codes and criteria for mental health diagnostic listings. These codes are filed with insurance claims. Work is underway on DSM-IV, which is expected to be published in early 1994.

ERISA (Employee Retirement Income Security Act): Federal law that allows self-insured companies to structure health benefits, including mental health benefits, as they wish and not be subject to state insurance mandates. An *ERISA plan* is an employer health insurance plan that is self-funded by the employer although often administered by an administrator such as an insurance company.

Exclusions: Defined illnesses, procedures, or circumstances such as preexisting conditions that are not subject to reimbursement in an insurance contract.

Extraterritoriality: An exception to state insurance mandates that permits companies located in multiple states to supersede state laws allowing the laws of the state in which the insurance contract was signed to be preeminent.

Federal Employees' Health Benefits (FEHB) Program: The plethora of group health plans or insurers that cover federal employees and contract employees.

Freedom of Choice: State laws that provide reimbursement for mental health services to a variety of health care practitioners and thus give the client the freedom to choose.

Health Maintenance Organization (HMO): An organization that provides all the care a patient needs for a fixed monthly price. Practitioners are paid on a capitated or discounted fee basis.

Health Care Financing Administration (HCFA): The federal agency that formulates policy and administers federal health programs.

HCFA-1500: The insurance claim form developed by HCFA. This is required for Medicare and other insurance companies.

Indemnity Carrier: A traditional health insurance company that sells insurance purchased by or for individuals or groups where the outright risk of health payment is incumbent upon the carrier. Usually the insured pays the carrier premiums based on previous actuarial usage.

International Classifications of Diseases, 9th Edition (ICD-9-CM): International diagnostic listings categorized by the World Health Organization. The codes are similar to those of *DSM-III-R*. Some insurance companies require *ICD-9-CM* codings and most accept them.

Managed Care: A concept applying to the provision of health care with a high level of utilization review. Managed care usually operates in conjunction with employers or other groups and their insurance carriers, which manage (fiscally) the health care of the group. Practitioners are usually paid on a discounted basis.

Major Medical: An additional provision to hospitalization and medical service policies that adds hospital days, amounts of medical services, and additional services as items the major medical portion will reimburse. Outpatient mental health services are often covered under the major medical portion of a contract.

Mandated Benefits: Health benefits required by law to be provided to the insured.

Medicaid: A federal and state program designed to provide health care coverage to lower income individuals. Medicaid regulations can vary from state to state.

Medical Necessity: Demonstrated medical criteria in order for services rendered to qualify for health care reimbursement.

Medicare: The federal health care program designed to provide reimbursement for health services to persons 65 years of age and older in addition to persons with severe disabilities. Part A covers hospital fees; Part B reimburses for practitioners fees.

Participating Provider: A practitioner who agrees to treat patients enrolled in a given program and who usually also agrees to accept the insurance company's set reimbursement (UCR) and receive payment directly from the insurance carrier instead of reimbursement through the client.

Policy Limitations: Criteria established by insurance carriers to limit the amount of reimbursable dollars per contract year or life of the contract for certain services or diagnostic codes.

Preexisting Condition: A medical condition possessed by the insured prior to the initiation of the insurance policy. Such a condition is usually not covered by insurance until a certain time period has elapsed.

Professional Counselor: A practitioner licensed to provide a variety of counseling-related services with specific duties and limitations varying from state to state. (See Counselor.) In some states, counseling professionals are regulated with titles such as Licensed Mental Health Counselor, Certified Practicing Counselor, or Certified Professional Counselor.

Preferred Provider Organization (PPO): An organization of practitioners in which participating providers agree to see certain patients for a discounted amount. Unlike an HMO, most PPO panels are open to any provider willing to accept the PPO's stipulations.

Primary Carrier: In coordination-of-benefit situations, the carrier with the responsibility of first payment.

Regulatory Board: A state entity that licenses, oversees, and disciplines providers in order to protect the public and regulate the professional discipline.

Scope of Practice: Definition of counselor's legal professional activities and limitations.

Secondary Carrier: The carrier in a coordinated benefits situation that reimburses after the first carrier has fulfilled obligations of the contract.

Self-Insured Company: An employer that sets aside a pool of funds to pay for the health expenses of its employees. Often such a company hires an administrator in the form of another insurance carrier to administer its program. Such companies are exempt from state insurance mandates. (See Administrator and ERISA.)

Unofficial Payment: Payment rendered to a practitioner by an insurance company in conflict with that insurance company's regulations. Also referred to as *Accidental Reimbursement*.

Usual, Customary, and Reasonable (UCR): A fee computed and established by an insurance carrier as the maximum allowable amount the company will pay for certain procedures based upon practitioner, diagnostic code, or procedure performed. Hypothetically, this is computed as the average fee charged for the procedure in a given geographical area.

 # Introduction to Third-Party Reimbursers

What is a *third-party reimburser*? The first party is the client, the second party is the mental health services provider, and the third party usually is an insurance company. The third party reimburses a policyholder for the cost of services rendered by a practitioner. The third party can also be an employer, friend, or a governmental agency or program. Traditionally, health care reimbursement has been only for the services of physicians as they have treated medical problems. In 1973, New Jersey passed what is known as a *freedom-of-choice law*. This type of law requires insurance companies that reimburse physicians for mental health services to also reimburse other specified practitioners who are qualified to render the same services. Since 1973, freedom-of-choice laws have been enacted in at least 40 states (Small, 1991; Stromberg et al., 1988; Whiting, 1989).

Only recently have the clients of professional counselors enjoyed reimbursement for counseling services. In fact, insurance reimbursement for all types of mental health services provided by a variety of practitioners (including physicians) has occurred only in the last 25 to 30 years with any degree of regularity, with a rapid increase of reimbursement for mental health services occurring during the 1970s.

Seldom has outpatient mental health coverage been reimbursed in its entirety. It has usually been reimbursed on a percentage basis under the client's major medical contract, with the percentage of the client's copay traditionally being 20% but increasing to 50% in recent years. In fact, mental health coverage appears to be under attack by state legislators and employers in efforts to curtail the growth of rapidly increasing health care costs. With these trends, where does the professional counselor fit?

Many mental health practitioners see reimbursement issues as unprofessional and mercenary (Small, 1991). Other professionals, often trained in more traditional settings, see the inclusion of third-party issues as tainting the therapeutic relationship. These therapeutic purists often insist that payment for services be an issue strictly between therapist and client and refuse to get involved in insurance reimbursement issues. Some mental health practitioners expect payment in full at the time of the session regardless of third-party payment and will not themselves file for insurance reimbursement. The matter of trying to gain insurance reimbursement is left to the client. Some practitioners have developed cash-only practices.

Kovacs (1988) advocated establishing mental health services as human services similar to those services provided by professionals such as lawyers, financial planners, architects, and accountants. He noted that the services of these professions are paid for by the general public and are seen as "important, significant, even vital. . .and well worth paying for." These professions obviously do well financially without benefit of insurance reimbursement, although many properly note that the poor do not have equal access to these uninsured services. Similarly, certain medical specialties cater to wealthier individuals, and those care providers actually prefer not to be limited by insurance, with its attendant UCR limitations. Plastic surgery is an example. Although Kovacs' advocacy of uninsured mental health services is thought provoking and a situation that eventually could become reality if the mental health third-party reimbursement bubble bursts, for now health insurance remains the only way many people can afford mental health services. Further, if health care reform in the 1990s leads to universal health insurance, it is clear that mental health practitioners will be forced to cope with the insurance culture into the foreseeable future. Indeed, it appears that mental health services will continue to be reimbursed under health insurance plans, and that the people needing these services as well as the livelihoods of mental health practitioners will be dependent upon third-party reimbursement.

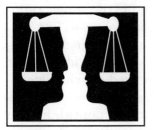

Professional Counselors and Third-Party Reimbursement

Highlights in the history of third-party payment regulations with regard to licensed professional counselors. Include the following:

- CHAMPUS recognizes marriage, family, child, and pastoral counselors—1974. To gain reimbursement from CHAMPUS, the client must be referred by a physician and the treatment medically indicated and necessary to the health of the client.
- The United States Office of Personnel Management (OPM) lists professional counselors and other practitioners whose services will be reimbursed under the Federal Employees Health Benefits contracts—1980. Unfortunately, this recognition is limited to the states identified as having shortages in primary medical care. As of 1992, this policy is limited to five states.
- Licensed marriage, family, and child counselors in California are recognized as approved providers for mental health services if the client is referred from a physician—1981.
- Blue Cross/Blue Shield of Southwest Virginia begins reimbursing licensed professional counselors if the client is

referred from a physician—1982. Referral must be deemed a medical necessity and associated with treatment provided by the referring physician.

- Professional counselors in Florida are included as recognized practitioners eligible for health insurance reimbursement—1983.
- Blue Cross/Blue Shield of Virginia begins offering an optional rider for subscribers providing for the direct reimbursement of licensed professional counselors—1984.
- Professional counselors in Colorado are recognized as reimbursable practitioners if services are provided under the supervision of a physician or licensed psychologist—1984.
- Professional counselors in community mental health centers are recognized as reimbursable practitioners by Medicaid—1984. Reimbursement, however, is provided to the community mental health center directly and not to the client or counselor rendering the service. Medicaid providers must meet minimal education requirements, do not need to be licensed in the state in which they operate, and must practice under the supervision of a psychiatrist.
- Montana mandates third-party reimbursement for the services of professional counselors (Covin, 1990a)—1985.
- Blue Shield of California begins to reimburse licensed marriage, family, and child counselors, providing the client was referred by a physician (Covin, 1990a)—1985.
- Professional counselors in Virginia are included in the Virginia freedom-of-choice code as reimbursable practitioners in all health insurance policies issued within that state (Covin, 1990a)—1987.
- CHAMPUS includes Certified Clinical Mental Health Counselors (CCMHC) as practitioners eligible for reimbursement (Covin, 1990a)—1987.
- Professional counselors in Colorado are included in the state statutes as reimbursable practitioners in all health insurance contracts written in that state, providing that the client was referred by a psychologist or physician and the professional counselor was supervised by a physician or psychologist—1988.

- Professional counselors in Vermont become eligible for inclusion as reimbursable practitioners in health insurance contracts written in that state (Covin, 1990a)—1988.
- Licensed professional counselors in Texas gain inclusion in that state's freedom-of-choice code by being named as eligible practitioners for reimbursement, providing the referral from a physician precedes treatment (Covin, 1990a)—1989.
- Blue Cross/Blue Shield of North Carolina includes counselors in its health insurance contracts, providing that the counselor is an employee of an eligible psychologist or physician (Covin, 1990a)—1989.
- Licensed professional counselors in Michigan gain recognition as reimbursable practitioners as Blue Cross/Blue Shield of Michigan is required to include licensed professional counselors as reimbursable providers in its health insurance contracts (Covin, 1990a)—1989.
- Marriage, family, and child counselors in Connecticut gain inclusion in state statutes as reimbursable practitioners (Covin, 1990a)—1992.
- Employees of the state of Oregon were given the right to receive mental health services from licensed professional counselors and have the services reimbursed under a Blue Cross/Blue Shield benefit plan—1992.
- Licensed professional counselors are included as reimbursable practitioners in the freedom-of-choice code in Mississippi—1992.

As of 1993, nine states mandate coverage for reimbursement for professional counselors (California, Colorado, Connecticut, Florida, Maryland, New Hampshire, Mississippi, Texas, and Virginia). The mandates vary from state to state.

As professional counselors continue attempts to gain recognition as health care providers, to secure insurance mandates in all states, and to better define their role, one difficulty they must face is the trend in the insurance industry to scale down coverage. Another difficulty is that professional counselors have only been licensed in various states since the 1970s. Thus many legislators, insurance companies, and others must be educated as to the qualifications, scope of practice, and contributions that professional counselors have to offer the health care system. Compounding the problem is the lack of uniform standards from state to state on training, credentialing, expertise, and scope of practice.

Covin (1992) discussed the wide diversity among the 35 state counselor regulatory laws. There are 11 different title descriptions for those who practice counseling throughout the United States where counselor regulatory laws exist: licensed professional counselor, mental health counselor, registered professional counselor, certified professional counselor, certified counselor of mental health, certified mental health counselor, licensed mental health counselor, certified counselor, certified clinical mental health counselor, licensed clinical professional counselor, and marriage, family, and child counselor. For the professions of psychiatry, nursing, psychology, and social work, one title description is used basically across all 50 states.

Covin (1992) also related that among the 35 state regulatory statutes, education requirements range from a minimum of a 30-semester-hour graduate degree to a specific comprehensive 60-semester-hour master's degree. In addition, many counselors with far less than the minimum requirements have been grandfathered into licensure because they were essentially practicing before stricter regulations were enacted. Further, most counseling laws contain exclusions that allow individuals to practice the profession of counseling outside of regulation. Many states allow anyone to practice counseling as long as the practitioner does not use the term *licensed counselor,* and in many states, counselors employed by community mental health centers, state hospitals, and nonprofit organizations as well as employee assistance programs are exempt from licensure.

Covin (1992) related that the state statutes defining the scope of practice and the definition of counseling itself are different in virtually each state with licensure certification and registration laws:

> Counseling is not recognized as a unified or uniformly qualified profession within the mental health provider community and third-party industry. Therefore, counselors are routinely being excluded as approved providers by an ever-growing majority of organizations which help pay for patient services. (p. 3)

Why Professional Counselors Sometimes Are Not Reimbursed

Professional counselors are not reimbursed sometimes because of state law, insurance regulations, exemptions to state law, Medicaid/Medicare, "accidental" reimbursement, the counselor's lack of insurance sophistication, error/deletion, and preexisting conditions.

1. State Law

As already noted, nine states mandate insurance reimbursement for professional counselors. In the remaining states, state law lists other practitioners in freedom-of-choice laws or makes no provision for the reimbursement of professional counselors. Most states stipulate the scope of practice for certain mental health practitioners. In these circumstances, professional counselors often are excluded from performing services that are insurance reimbursable. For example, in some states the practice of *psychotherapy* is specifically and exclusively reserved for practitioners other than counselors. The provision of *coun-*

seling per se is usually not deemed reimbursable by insurance carriers.

2. Insurance Regulations

Most insurance carriers establish a list of reimbursable practitioners. In states where freedom-of-choice codes apply, insurance companies include all practitioners listed under the law. In states without freedom-of-choice statutes, the insurance carrier establishes its own approved list of practitioners. By virtue of issues already discussed, often professional counselors are not included in these lists of providers. With a significant number of companies, reimbursement for professional counselors is provided only when under the supervision of another recognized and identified practitioner such as a psychiatrist or clinical psychologist.

Many insurance carriers establish, using their own criteria, certain procedures or diagnostic codes that are not reimbursable. It is known that some carriers will not reimburse for marital or family therapy unless there is an identified patient with a diagnosable medical condition (*DSM-III-R* or *ICD-9-CM*). Furthermore, the procedure must be addressing the identified diagnostic code in order to be reimbursed. Marital or family therapy conducted to improve the relationship is seen by many carriers as a social versus medical problem, and because the problem is not medical, health insurance reimbursement is seen as inappropriate. Biofeedback is another procedure usually not reimbursed.

Many insurance carriers, using their own criteria, have deemed that certain diagnostic codes are not reimbursable. Recent *DSM-III-R* diagnostic codes that are apparently under scrutiny and often are not reimbursed are:

    antisocial personality disorders (301.7)
    inadequate personality (301.6)
    sexual deviation (302.1-302.4, 302.8-302.84, 302.89-302.9)
    autistic disease of childhood (299.0)
    mental retardation (317-319)
    learning disabilities (315-315.2)
    tobacco abuse (305.1)

conduct and oppositional disorders (312-312.9, 313.81) (United Behavioral Systems, Inc., personal communication, November 4, 1991).

Policies vary from company to company, and these policies often change without notice. But whatever the insurance carrier's policy, the professional counselor should be entirely truthful as to the procedure performed and the medical or other circumstances surrounding the treatment. An accurate diagnosis should be rendered regardless of whether it is a diagnosis that is deemed to be reimbursable by the particular insurance company involved.

Health insurance contracts exist for the reimbursement of practitioners treating essentially medical problems as defined by established diagnostic criteria. As such, the professional counselor should recognize that many clients may not meet the definition of *medical necessity* in order to qualify for reimbursement. *DSM-III-R* lists some diagnoses as "conditions not attributable to a mental disorder." Such conditions are known as *V-codes* because the letter *V* precedes the numbers in the code. *DSM-III-R* defines V-codes as "a behavioral or psychological problem that may appropriately be a focus of professional attention or treatment even though it is not attributable to a mental disorder." Such codes include:

V-62.30 - academic problem
V-71.01 - adult antisocial behavior
V-71.02 - childhood or adolescent antisocial behavior
V-65.20 - malingering
V-61.10 - marital problem
V-15.81 - noncompliance with medical treatment
V-62.20 - occupational problem
V-61.20 - parent/child problem
V-62.81 - other interpersonal problem
V-61.80 - other specified family circumstances
V-62.89 - phase of life problem or other life circumstance
            problem
V-62.82 - uncomplicated bereavement
V-71.09 - no diagnosis or condition on Axis I
V-71.09 - no diagnosis or condition on Axis II

3. Exemptions to State Law

Even in states where reimbursement for clients of professional counselors is mandated, certain exemptions to the law may exist. The three most prominent exceptions are extraterritoriality, self-insured plans, and federal plans:

- **Extraterritoriality**. This is a situation in which a company operating in a state with mandates can bypass those mandates by signing a contract with an insurance carrier in another state in which that company operates that does not have the same mandates. In 1992, only 16 states have specific extraterritoriality laws prohibiting this practice. Thus, if a mandate in state X requires clients of professional counselors to be reimbursed, a company with corporate offices in state Y, which may not have an insurance mandate, can sign that contract in state Y, thus dictating to the employees in state X that they will be subject to state Y regulations. As such, the employees in state X do not have available to them reimbursable care from a professional counselor despite laws that mandate this occurring. Currently, the states that possess extraterritoriality laws are Arkansas, California, Hawaii, Maryland, Massachusetts, New Hampshire, New Jersey, New York, North Carolina, Ohio, Oklahoma, Texas, Utah, and Wyoming. Of these states, California and Texas are the only states in which professional counselors enjoy both mandated freedom of choice and extraterritoriality protection (Covin, 1990a).
- **Self-Insured Plans**. An increasing number of employers, in an effort to curtail rising health care costs and to avoid insurance mandates, set aside a sum of money to pay for the medical claims of their employees. Often the employer hires an administrator or fiduciary, which is usually an established insurance carrier, to administer the processing of claims and the payment for these claims. Often the administrator or fiduciary has established criteria as to providers who are reimbursable for specified services. These plans are exempt from state mandates because such plans are classified as *employee welfare benefit plans* and are regulated by a federal law known as the Employee Retire-

ment Income Securities Act (ERISA). Professional counselors and other practitioners are sometimes omitted by such plans.
* **Federal Plans.** Federal employees have approximately 140 insurance plans from which to choose (Covin, 1990b). Benefits vary from contract to contract. These plans are administered by a wide range of insurance entities that administer the plans, including Blue Cross/Blue Shield, Mailhandlers, American Federation of Government Employees, GEHA, National Association of Letter Carriers, and Aetna (Covin, 1990b). More than 10 million federal employees are enrolled in these programs (Small, 1991).

Regardless of a state's law, employees of the United States Government are subject to health care regulations established in Washington, D.C. As of 1992, most federal plans, with the exception of CHAMPUS, exclude payment for the services of professional counselors. A rejection of such a claim is often confusing to the counselor who might see that the claim itself is being submitted to an insurance company that has traditionally paid for the professional counselor's services. As in the case of a self-insured plan, the federal government often contracts with local or regional carriers to administer the federal program. In such cases, the regulations of the federal government supersede state law.

An exception exists for licensed professional counselors that allows reimbursement in states currently identified by the U.S. Office of Personnel Management (OPS) as having shortages in medical practitioners. Presently, professional counselors in Alabama, Louisiana, Mississippi, West Virginia, and Wyoming are eligible for reimbursement (Covin, 1990b).

4. Medicaid/Medicare

At the present time, direct payment to professional counselors under Medicare is not allowed. Specific issues will be discussed in the next chapter.

State Medicaid law varies, but in most situations professional counselors are excluded. Counselors operating in community mental health centers who are employed by the centers are eligible for unofficial or accidental reimbursement. However, the reimbursement itself is paid directly to the center, and the services must be rendered under the supervision of a psychiatrist.

In the past, professional counselors and other practitioners who were ineligible for direct Medicare or Medicaid reimbursement have worked under the supervision of a reimbursable practitioner (such as a psychiatrist) in order to be reimbursed for their services. This practice has come under increased scrutiny, and counselors should be wary of various state Medicaid regulations regarding this practice. Counselors are advised to investigate state regulations before embarking on such an arrangement because in most cases this practice is now deemed illegal.

Professional counselors may be eligible for Medicare reimbursement while working under the supervision of a recognized reimbursable practitioner if certain conditions are met. These conditions are discussed in the next chapter.

5. "Accidental" Reimbursement

Counselors are sometimes reimbursed by "accident," receiving payment when the carrier's policies prohibit payment to professional counselors. Thus a counselor might hear another counselor say, "Well, insurance company so and so paid me." This can be confusing because the counselor may have just had a claim rejected by that same company. Remember that insurance claims are processed by clerks responsible for processing a large volume under time pressures. Most insurance clerks are not versed in mental health issues. A clerk seeing *PhD* and not reading *professional counselor* may automatically assume that the PhD is a clinical psychologist and approve the reimbursement. Often decisions are made to reimburse without thoroughly reviewing the claim submitted, and in the process, the clients of many professional counselors are reimbursed contrary to insurance policies prohibiting this reimbursement. Professional counselors should not assume that because their clients have been reimbursed by a certain company that a conscious decision has been made to start reimbursing for the services of professional counselors based on any kind of logic whatsoever. In situations where reimbursement has not been either arranged, negotiated, or mandated by law, the professional counselor should not be surprised if a later claim is rejected.

6. Counselor Lack of Insurance Sophistication

Often claims are rejected because they lack basic, yet vital detail. Professional counselors should be familiar with the Codes in CPT-4 *(Physicians Current Procedural Terminology)* that ascribes code numbers to various procedures including psychotherapy and psychological testing. Additionally, the professional counselor submitting a claim should render an accurate diagnosis code from either *DSM-III-R* or *ICD-9-CM* depending upon the requirements of the insurance company. This diagnosis should accurately reflect the clinical presentation of the client and should not be altered simply to gain reimbursement.

A professional counselor should not bill for services that he or she is not adequately trained to render. A professional counselor should also be honest in filing a health insurance claim, and the claim should reflect precisely the procedures rendered and the diagnosis code. For example, a counselor should not bill for psychotherapy when career counseling has actually been rendered.

7. Error/Deletion

Expect most claims that delete essential information or contain incorrect information to be automatically rejected.

8. Preexisting Conditions

Many insurance carriers will not reimburse for mental health services when a subscriber is new to the company and has a history of mental health treatment until the subscriber has been enrolled in the health plan for a minimum period of time. This time varies but is usually 6 to 12 months after first enrolling in the health care plan.

9. Policy Exclusions

In states without mandates or when exceptions to mandates apply, some insurance policies will not reimburse for mental health services of any kind, by any provider.

10. Late Filing

Most insurance carriers reject claims filed after a certain amount of time has passed from the date of services.

Major Health Reimbursement Plans

Blue Cross/Blue Shield, Civilian Health and Medical Program of the Uniformed Services (CHAMPUS), Medicare, Medicaid, and Federal Employees Health Benefits Program are among major health reimbursement plans. Others are provided by private insurers and self-insured companies.

Blue Cross and Blue Shield

The concept of health insurance, with fees for medical services paid in exchange for monthly payments from the subscriber, allegedly began in Texas in 1929 when a hospital offered to provide teachers 20 days of hospital care for 50 cents a month. Since then health insurance has proliferated. Hospitals offering insurance formed networks, and eventually Blue Cross/Blue Shield was formed (Pennsylvania Blue Shield, 1989). As of 1988, Blue Cross/Blue Shield companies provided hospitalization insurance to approximately one third of Americans and coverage for physicians to approximately one quarter of Americans (Stromberg et al., 1988).

Blue Cross/Blue Shield plans are found almost nationwide, but their policies, coverage, and share of the marketplace varies. Each Blue Cross and Blue Shield organization is separate from the other. Often there are several Blue Cross/Blue Shield plans in a state, each with different policies regarding the services of professional counselors in the absence of mandated coverage. For example, Pennsylvania has four separate regional Blue Cross organizations and one statewide Blue Shield plan (Small, 1991).

An example of the potential problems professional counselors may experience based on the part of the state in which they practice comes from Virginia, where before 1987 there were three Blue Cross plans. In 1983, Blue Cross/Blue Shield of Southwest Virginia chose to recognize licensed professional counselors as approved providers of mental health care in the treatment of mental and emotional disorders. Blue Cross/Blue Shield of Virginia, the larger of the two plans, opted to provide for the services of professional counselors only when the subscriber purchased an additional optional rider at an additional cost. Blue Cross/Blue Shield of the Capitol D.C. area, located in Northern Virginia, chose not to reimburse counselors in any way.

In 1986, Blue Cross/Blue Shield of Virginia and Blue Cross/Blue Shield of Southwest Virginia merged. The fate of reimbursement for counselors was in question. Due to the lobbying efforts of the Virginia Association of Clinical Counselors, a branch of the American Mental Health Counselors Association, the merged Blue Cross/Blue Shield of Virginia recognized professional counselors as reimbursable practitioners on a voluntary basis in 1986. Further, Blue Cross/Blue Shield, a very powerful legislative force in Virginia, did not lobby against legislative efforts to include professional counselors in the freedom-of-choice code, and professional counselors were included in the code in July 1987. The Blue Cross/Blue Shield plan of the Capitol D.C. area chose not to recognize professional counselors in the freedom-of-choice code; and only after a State Corporation Commission ruling in 1989 did the organization finally capitulate and begin reimbursing professional counselors.

Professional counselors should be aware that Blue Cross reimburses for hospital expenses, and that Blue Shield reimburses for the services of the practitioner. Many Blue Shield plans, however, do not pay for outpatient psychotherapy. Psychotherapy is often reimbursed through a major medical plan, which is usually part of the Blue Cross/Blue Shield contract. In rare instances, a major medical plan might be purchased from a second company.

Many Blue Cross/Blue Shield plans have what is known as *participating providers.* A participating provider is a practitioner who agrees to accept as full payment the established Blue Cross/Blue Shield usual, customary, and reasonable (UCR) fee for that particular type of practitioner and for the *CPT-4* procedure provided. If a practitioner participates, the Blue Cross/ Blue Shield reimbursement check goes directly to the participating provider.

When the provider does not participate, the provider is free to charge the client whatever rate he or she chooses. The rate of reimbursement, however, from Blue Cross/Blue Shield will only be a percentage based on the patient's policy (50% or 80%) of the UCR. Additionally, in situations in which the practitioner does not participate the reimbursement check from Blue Cross/ Blue Shield goes directly to the client. Unfortunately, many of these checks never reach the provider.

The UCR is computed by each particular Blue Cross/Blue Shield plan based upon the license of the practitioner, the geographical area, and the procedure performed.

Blue Cross/Blue Shield participating provider agreements vary from plan to plan. However, it should be reiterated that the participating professional counselor must accept the Blue Shield payment as full payment and may not bill for more than the allowed fee. Remember that payment from Blue Cross/ Blue Shield will only be a percentage of the UCR. The counselor can collect the client's copay but *cannot* charge over the UCR if participating.

Whether or not a counselor becomes a participating provider is clearly the option of the provider. In states where there is no freedom-of-choice law that includes professional counselors, this may not be an option. In some areas, being a participating provider could provide a competitive edge over nonparticipating providers. In any case, this decision is similar to deciding whether or not to participate in a managed care system, which usually involves the acceptance of discounted fees in return for referrals and direct reimbursement.

As already stated, each Blue Cross/Blue Shield plan is a separate entity that does and can establish its own rules and regulations within state laws and guidelines. Blue Cross/Blue Shield plans have been noted nationwide as having their own idiosyncratic policies related to mental health treatment. Thus it is the responsibility of professional counselors to familiarize themselves with the Blue Cross/Blue Shield plans that may be operating in the areas professional counselors serve.

CHAMPUS (Civilian Health and Medical Program of the Uniformed Services)

CHAMPUS is the largest health insurance plan in the United States, covering more than 8.5 million people (Small, 1991). Clients with CHAMPUS coverage are mostly found in areas surrounding large military installations. For counselors in such areas, obtaining CHAMPUS reimbursement is vital to their livelihood.

CHAMPUS is known for having made more professions eligible for reimbursement, including certain counselors, than most other government programs. In order for a professional counselor to be eligible for reimbursement by CHAMPUS, the professional counselor must possess the following:

> (1) Minimum of master's degree in mental health counseling or allied mental health field from a regionally accredited institution; (2) Two years of postmaster's experience which includes 3,000 hours of clinical work and 100 hours of face-to-face supervision; (3) Licensed and certified to practice as a marriage and family counselor, pastoral counselor, or mental health counselor by the jurisdiction where practicing; or if the jurisdiction does not provide for licensure or certification, is certified by or is eligible for membership in the appropriate national or professional association that sets standards for the profession. (Office of Civilian Health and Medical Program of the Uniformed Services [CHAMPUS], 1988)

In order for CHAMPUS to reimburse, the client must be referred by a physician. The physician must actually see the patient initially, perform an evaluation, and arrive at an initial diagnostic impression prior to the referral to the counselor. The physician must also provide "oversight" and "supervision" of the treatment (CHAMPUS, 1988). It is suggested that oversight and supervision consist of regular, documented discussions between the referring physician and the professional counselor and that the counselor and physician send chart notes after each contact to the other.

In 1991, CHAMPUS began more closely scrutinizing the credentials of counselors. Certain practitioners with an MEd degree were denied reimbursement on the assumption that the degree was primarily educational and not clinical. Those practitioners holding MEd degrees who were able to prove their programs were counseling in nature were recognized as providers by CHAMPUS.

According to CHAMPUS:

> ...because of the diverse degrees we are seeing from applicants in the field of mental health counseling (as well as marriage and family counseling), we are indeed finding it necessary to look beyond the title of the degree to determine the course content. . . .
>
> We are seeing individuals apply for CHAMPUS certification with such diverse graduate degrees as sociology, anthropology, or dance. In some cases, these individuals are being licensed or certified by the state as a mental health provider. We are very concerned about the ability of individuals with this type of educational background to render psychotherapy to individuals with a diagnosed mental disorder. Unfortunately, there are no clear-cut national guidelines for counselors as to the type of degrees or course work considered appropriate, as there are for other mental health professions. (CHAMPUS, personal communication, December 17, 1991)

Medicare

Medicare legislation was established in 1965 as a part of President Lyndon Johnson's Great Society. It is a federal program to provide health services to United States citizens 65 and older who are eligible for other Social Security benefits and, in addition, to pay for the health care of individuals who are deemed disabled under Social Security requirements. Medicare currently insures approximately 30 million individuals (Small, 1991). Strong has suggested that developments in Medicare are of utmost importance to all mental health practitioners because other insurance carriers use Medicare as a model, and federal, state, and private plans often use the same language as Medicare. Small and others have suggested that Medicare is likely to be the model for any future national health insurance.

Medicare is administered by the Health Care Financing Administration (HCFA). HCFA contracts with private insurance companies to process Medicare claims. As such, these private carriers are similar to other insurance carriers that contract with self-insured plans and other federal programs to administer the larger federal Medicare program.

There are two aspects of Medicare: Part A is a program available to all eligible individuals. Individuals do not pay a premium for Part A. Part A covers hospital care and nursing facilities. The services of mental health practitioners are generally not reimbursed under Part A.

Part B, also known as *supplementary medical insurance,* is an optional coverage that involves the Medicare recipient paying a monthly premium. Most Part A enrollees also subscribe to Part B (Stromberg et al., 1988). Until July 1, 1990, only physicians were eligible for reimbursement for mental health services under Medicare Part B. Psychologists could obtain reimbursement only for psychological testing and only if referred by a physician. No other mental health practitioners were eligible for reimbursement (Small, 1991).

A bill passed by Congress in 1989 required Medicare to reimburse both psychologists and social workers for outpatient mental health services. Psychologists and social workers are required to notify the client's primary physician after treatment has commenced unless the patient requests that this not occur. There are no provisions for reimbursement of other mental health practitioners, including professional counselors. Since the passage of the 1989 law, there has been a great deal of confusion because formulating the specific regulations to implement the law itself has been slow. It appears that professional counselors who have the desire to work with Medicare patients must affiliate themselves with either a physician, clinical psychologist, or social worker who is eligible for direct reimbursement from Medicare.

Such a supervisory arrangement cannot be taken lightly. Stringent efforts should insure that the supervisory arrangement meets Medicare requirements. In order for professional counselors to be eligible, the supervisory arrangement must meet Medicare *incident to services* standards. Incident to services can only be performed under the direct personal supervision of a clinical psychologist, social worker, or physician eligible for reimbursement under Medicare.

Incident to services are:

1. mental health services that are commonly furnished in physicians' offices.
2. an integral, although incidental, part of professional services performed by the clinical psychologist, physician, or clinical social worker.
3. performed under the direct supervision of the clinical psychologist, physician, or social worker. That is, the clinical psychologist, physician, or social worker *must be physically present and immediately available*.
4. performed by an employee of the clinical psychologist, social worker, or physician (or an employee of a legal entity that employs the supervisory clinician) (U.S. Department of Health and Human Services, 1990).

Significant limitations were placed upon the mental health benefits for Medicare recipients in the past, but as of July 1990, there is no annual dollar limit for Part B mental health services. All mental health benefits are subject to a 50% copayment but no annual limits (Small, 1991).

Medicare fees are computed in a very complicated manner. The *approved amount* is automatically reduced by 62.5%, creating an *allowed amount*. Medicare then reimburses 80% of the allowed amount (Small, 1991).

Small (1991) put forth the following hypothetical example:

Practitioners regular fee	$100.00
Medicare's approved amount	$ 80.00
Mental health limitations	62.5% (of amount approved)
Allowed amount	$ 50.00
Medicare payment x 80%	$ 40.00
Copayment from client	$ 40.00

Many Medicare recipients purchase what is known as Medi-Gap supplemental insurance. These policies reimburse the Medicare recipient for copayments and deductibles for which the recipient is responsible under Medicare regulations. These policies are usually purchased from private insurance carriers. When there is no reimbursement by Medicare, the Medi-Gap payment likewise pays nothing.

Medicaid

Medicaid was enacted by Congress in 1965 to pay medical expenses for low-income individuals who met certain criteria. Medicaid is administered by the federal government and individual states. The federal government places basic requirements for Medicaid, but each state or territory has its own version. There are currently 53 separate state and territorial programs involved in the administration of Medicaid nationwide (Koyanagi, 1988).

As such, there are many differences between the different programs based upon their objectives, philosophies, and certain needs of different territories and states. The laws are quite complex.

As noted in the last chapter, Medicaid does reimburse for the services of counselors operating in community mental health centers. Reimbursement is made directly to the community mental health center, and the services must be rendered under the supervision of a psychiatrist.

According to Small (1991):

> The federal government requires that Medicaid provide: (a) inpatient hospital services (except for mental disorders); (b) outpatient hospital services; (c) physician services (MD or DO); (d) laboratory and x-ray services; (e) skilled nursing facility services (other than care in an institution for mental disease); (f) early periodic screening diagnosis, and treatment services for children; (g) family planning services; and (h) nurse midwife services. (pp. 63–64)

Small (1991) also indicated, that:

> States may render: (a) services provided by professionals who are licensed as practitioners under state law (psychologists,

psychiatrist social workers, and other mental health professionals); (b) home health care (which can include mental health
services if provided by a home health agency that meets Medicare requirements, or furnished under the supervision of a
registered nurse and prescribed by a physician); (c) clinical
services furnished by or under the direction of a physician,
without regard to whether the clinic itself is administered by a
physician; (d) other diagnostic, screening, preventive, and reha-
bilitation services; (e) psychiatric inpatient hospital services
and nursing facility services for individuals age 65 and over in
an institution for mental diseases; (f) intermediate care facility
services for persons with mental retardation; (g) inpatient
psychiatric hospital services for individuals under the age of 22;
(h) any other medical care and any other type of remedial care
recognized under state law; (i) targeted case management; and
(j) a variety of other services such as dentistry and physical
therapy. (pp. 64–65)

Based upon the state, certain limitations on the amount of
psychotherapy are placed either on an annual or a lifetime
basis. Limitations can also include restrictions on the amount
of reimbursement by dollar ($500 per year), and in other states
certain non-MD practitioners receive less reimbursement than
physicians.

Regulations regarding supervision of nonrecognized practitioners working under the supervision of recognized Medicaid
practitioners vary from state to state, and once again counselors
are encouraged to examine and investigate Medicaid regulations in the state in which they practice thoroughly before
embarking on such a supervisory arrangement. In most cases,
such arrangements are deemed illegal.

Federal Employees Health Benefits (FEHB) Program

As noted in the Professional Counselors and Third-Party Reimbursement chapter, as of 1992 provisions are only made in five
states for the reimbursement of professional counselors by
federal health insurance plans. These states are Alabama,
Louisiana, Mississippi, West Virginia, and Wyoming.

Professional counselors not in these states are usually not
reimbursed under FEHB contracts. These professional counse-

lors should call the administrator of the FEHB contract held by the client seeking services in order to determine eligibility for reimbursement.

Criteria for reimbursement under FEHB contracts in the five states in which professional counselors are approved providers are that:

- Services provided must be within the scope of the professional counselors' qualifications, training, and expertise.
- Services must be psychotherapy in nature.
- Services provided must be related to the diagnosis and treatment of mental disorders listed in *DSM-III-R* (or *ICD-9-CM*). Exclusions in FEHB contracts include psychotherapy rendered for "V-codes, marital and family therapy, or any type of educational, recreational, or milieu therapy" (Covin, 1990b).

Other Private Insurers

As many as two thirds of people not in government programs may have their health insurance covered by Aetna, Metropolitan, Prudential, Travelers, Cigna, Equitable, and other commercial companies (Small, 1991). Most clients covered by private insurance carriers possess these policies as part of a company benefit plan.

Small (1991) listed the following characteristics of commercial insurers:

- Private insurance carriers often exclude services not ordered by a physician unless dictated by law.
- Most private insurance carriers enforce limitations on preexisting conditions. Usually insurance carriers will not pay for mental health services during the first year of coverage. On most insurance forms there is a question as to when the symptoms first appeared. The answer to this question might be used to determine a preexisting condition. Some insurance companies define a preexisting condition as one for which treatment was sought earlier during a designated period of time.

- Private insurance carriers will pay only for treatment that is medically necessary.
- Most inpatient mental health services are reimbursed at between 80 and 100% of the UCR.
- Private insurance usually pays for psychological testing, psychotherapy, and psychiatric/psychological consultations.
- Coverage for outpatient psychotherapy is less than for inpatient psychotherapy. Copayments range from 0 to 50%. Additionally, there is often a maximum allowable fee, sometimes as low as $20. In such situations a plan might pay a certain percent of the allowable charge. In some situations, a therapist may charge $80 for a session but only be reimbursed $20 as the contract called for 50% of the allowable fee, which in this case was established by the carrier at $40.
- Most private insurance carriers allow assignment and do not obligate the practitioner to accept the assignment as full fee.
- Most private insurers have annual deductibles that may be applied individually to each family member or to the family unit.
- Some private insurance carriers include caps. As such, a certain dollar amount may be set for the maximum allowable reimbursement per contract year for mental health services, or there may be a limit to the number of sessions reimbursed.

Self-Insured Companies

As noted in the preceding chapter, because of ERISA, companies that decide to set aside a certain dollar amount for medical claims and that hire insurance carriers to administer the program are exempt from any state mandates in terms of insurance coverage. It is our experience that few companies decide on their own what services will be covered and which practitioners reimbursed. When the self-insured company hires an administrator or fiduciary, the insurance carrier administering the program already has in its possession established criteria. The insurance carrier often applies these criteria nationwide with little regard for the insurance mandates in the states in which it operates. The professional counselor should remember that most probably the self-insured company hired the particular health insurance carrier to administer the program with the goal of minimizing to whatever degree possible the amount of money spent on medical claims. As such, the employer and the insurance carrier administering the self-insured plan may initially be reluctant to consider reimbursement for professional counselors on the automatic assumption that increasing the provider pool increases costs.

Professional counselors who are stymied by self-insured plans can directly approach the employer and ask that professional counselors be included in the reimbursable provider pool. It is our experience that often the insurance carrier administering the self-insured plan is responsive to a request by the employer. Conversely, professional counselors contacting the insurance carrier administering the program should expect a great deal more resistance.

Although ERISA regulations usually work to the detriment of the professional counselor, the professional counselor should remember that they can also work in his or her favor. Because of ERISA, employers are essentially free to do whatever they want to do and are not bound by state regulations regarding insurance. Therefore, professional counselors can and should approach the self-insured companies and offer their services as part of a PPO network, or an EAP plan, through an exclusive provider agreement with discounted fees, or by managing the inpatient and outpatient treatment of the employees in conjunction with the insurance carrier administering the program.

Legal Issues

Important legal issues for counselors in relation to third-party payments are counselor regulation and licensure, state insurance statutes, insurance fraud, and malpractice.

Counselor Regulation and Licensure

The laws of most states are premised upon the simple concept that unless an activity or profession is specifically regulated it is unregulated. When a profession or activity is unregulated, no state license is required, no permission from a government entity is needed to conduct that profession or activity.

The purpose of licensing, is to assure that the activity being regulated is of good quality and that the public is protected. When a profession is licensed, part and parcel of that licensure is the setting of minimum standards for licensure and ongoing monitoring for quality problems. The practice of medicine by medical doctors is regulated specifically in all 50 states, for example. No person can practice medicine unless the person has a license or fits within some statutory exemption from licensure.

Counseling has traditionally not been specifically regulated, and for years the practice of counseling in one form or another has not required the permission of the government in the form of a license. An individual could go in the street, or into a church, or to a party and provide counseling at will without needing the permission of the state. However, recently states have begun to regulate counseling. During the early years of this regulation, grandfathering occurred, that is, certain individuals who today would not have the requisite academic or experience criteria for licensure were allowed to obtain licenses.

Should a profession invite regulation? Some counselors have opposed regulation because of the perception that the setting of minimum standards is arbitrary or excludes from licensure (and thus counseling) many competent professionals. But putting aside the issue of protecting the public, the simple and ironic truth is that professions that are highly regulated are more easily able to obtain third-party reimbursement. Indeed, the general policy of the Blue Shields across the country is to reimburse professional counselors only in those jurisdictions where they are licensed (assuming that the services are covered and medically necessary). Unlicensed counselors are not eligible for Blue Shield reimbursement.

As noted in the Professional Counselors and Third-Party Reimbursement chapter, there is no uniform definition for *professional counselor*, and some of the legal definitions are not specific. In Virginia, for example, the original definition said that *"Professional counselor* means a person trained in counseling and guidance services with emphasis on individual and group guidance and counseling designed to assist individuals in achieving more effective personal, social, educational, and career development and adjustment" (Virginia Code Section 54.1-3500).*

This type of definition is so broad that the state is then required to list exemptions so that persons who are not professional counselors but whose conduct falls within the broad definition are not inadvertently regulated. Thus, for example, people who provide counseling in Virginia need not be licensed professional counselors if they (1) do not charge for advice, (2) are students, (3) are clergymen, (4) are employees or volunteers

---

* A new definition which is more clinically relevant and specific is in effect as of July 1, 1993.

with government-based or sponsored community action organizations, or (5) are personnel managers employed by firms.

Such exemptions are broad, and it is easy to see that many people may lawfully be in the practice of professional counseling without having a license simply by being part of one of the broad exceptions. However, once payment is sought for professional counseling, it is advantageous to be licensed as a professional counselor.

State Insurance Statutes

Medical reimbursement policies have historically been dominated by medical doctors and dentists. The Blue Cross/Blue Shield organizations were originally founded by physicians and, until recent years, have been mostly run by physicians. Thus the Blue Shield companies have traditionally reimbursed those utilizing physician and dental services but have not been as generous in reimbursement policies with respect to other health care providers. Similarly, commercial insurers have preferred to deal with medical doctors and dentists and have been resistant to the demands of other, competing health care providers for reimbursement.

In addition to being reluctant to reimburse health care providers who were not medical doctors or dentists, insurance companies have often been very conservative regarding the reimbursement of mental health benefits. Fortunately, with the exception of ERISA plans, insurance is a regulated industry. Insurance companies must file their plans with the respective state insurance offices, and these plans must be approved. In addition, states also have the power to require insurance companies to offer certain benefits or to prevent discrimination among providers. The result, at the prodding of consumer groups and the health care industry, has been the development of *mandated benefits*. The concept of mandated benefits applies in two ways: First, an insurance company is required to pay for a certain service if a claim for that service is made by a subscriber. For example, insurance companies are often required to reimburse their subscribers for certain kinds of prenatal care and drug and alcohol addiction treatment. Many states have mandated benefits that apply to the provision of counseling services. These mandated benefits have been required as a matter of social policy.

Second, mandated benefits require that if a service is a covered service under an insurance plan, the insurer must pay any licensed health care provider who provides that service. In other words, if certain mental health services are provided, and the insurer reimburses a psychiatrist for the services, then re-imbursement should be provided for psychologists, social workers, or professional counselors who render the same services.

The concept of mandated benefits is now under heavy attack in many state legislatures. Many Blue Cross/Blue Shield organizations have been lobbying to obtain the right to sell bare-bones insurance to the public. The argument made by the carriers is that mandated benefits have raised the price of insurance to exorbitant levels that are not affordable by many people. The result, they argue, is that a large portion of the population is needlessly uninsured. Blue Cross/Blue Shield and other carriers have argued that they can produce an affordable product if they are allowed to sell bare-bones insurance without mandates. Mandates requiring parity among the professions as well as the provision of certain psychological services have been dropped from many bare-bones policies. Ironically, bare-bones policies have not been selling well, although their cost is as much as 50% below the price of the regular policies.

Preliminary studies by the Virginia Bureau of Insurance (in January 1993) indicated that the cost of mandating providers is only between 2 and 3% of total cost, depending on the policy type. Moreover, the claims experience for mandated providers is less than 1% on individual policies and less than 3% on group policies.

Professional counselors have to deal with both issues in the debate over bare-bones policies. Professional counselors—together with psychiatrists, psychologists, and others—need to defend the mandates for coverage of certain mental health services. Additionally, professional counselors need to defend their right to be paid if other practitioners are also paid for the same service.

Many insurance companies, particularly commercial carriers and newly formed managed health care plans, are not familiar with the mandated benefits and antidiscrimination laws in state jurisdictions. A professional counselor may have a legal right to be reimbursed, but insurance companies may not know of that right. The professional counselor should keep copies of antidiscrimination statutes and mandated benefits statutes and forward copies to reluctant insurance companies. If professional counselors are not aware of the statutes that apply to insurance reimbursement in their jurisdiction, they should immediately contact their state association and learn about those statutes.

Insurance Fraud

Quite simply, insurance fraud means obtaining money from an insurance company by lies or deception. In ordinary times, the commission of insurance fraud is legally and morally wrong. In these days of heightened utilization review, stepped-up insurance fraud prosecutions, and increased involvement of state licensure agencies in cracking down on insurance fraud, practicing insurance fraud is also professionally suicidal. Violators are almost always caught. Evidence of insurance fraud is easy to find in the medical records and easy to prove but very difficult to defend. The results of criminal or administration conviction are catastrophic and may bring professional or personal ruin.

There are several types of fraud in the provision of mental health services. Typical among them are misstatement of services, phantom visits, misrepresentation of the service provider, false representation of *CPT* codes or *DSM-III-R* diagnoses, charging insurance carriers for failed appointments, and charging lower fees for clients who do not have insurance.

Misstatement of services. Many insurance policies have exact limitations upon the amount of service that will be covered. A typical policy might only allow, for example, two visits per week. One type of fraud involves misrepresenting the number of visits and the length of visits. For example, a practitioner could file claims for two visits per week (the maximum allowed), each visit allegedly for an hour and a half, when, in fact, there

were four visits for 45 minutes each. A practitioner will sometimes rationalize that because the amount of time being claimed
is in the aggregate the same, the insurance company really does
not "lose anything." This logic is wrong. The insurance company
is being deceived out of money. Were the insurance company
told that there were four short visits instead of two long ones,
it would have paid only for two short visits (there being a
limitation of two per week).

Phantom visits. Another problem is when practitioners
make up phantom visits for billing purposes. This typically
happens with the practitioner whose bookkeeping methods are
particularly sloppy. Again, the rationale often is "I know I spent
a lot of time with this client that I did not keep track of, and the
extra visit that I am billing for makes up for that lost time." This
rationale is faulty. Indeed, practitioners who have tried to bill
insurance carriers using this rationale have gone to jail. The
reason is that when the insurance company is lied to about the
amount and timing of visits, it is denied the opportunity to
contest the billing, or to use its own methods to analyze medical
necessity.

Misrepresentation of the service provider. Sometimes
an insurance policy will cover mental health services when
provided by a psychiatrist or psychologist but not when provided
by a health care practitioner who is neither of these. A fraudu-
lent situation exists when a noncovered provider bills under a
doctor's name. For example, the insurance company is presented a bill for psychotherapy reported to be done by Dr. Jones
but in fact was provided by unlicensed intern Mr. Smith. The
insurance company assumes that the service was provided by
Dr. Jones and reimburses on that basis. By lying to the insurance company about who provided the service, providers are
obtaining reimbursement otherwise not allowable, or perhaps
obtaining reimbursement at a higher rate than might otherwise
obtain. This is fraud.

**False representation of *CPT-4* codes or *DSM-III-R* diag-
noses**. As noted before, some conditions are covered by insurance and some are not. It is not uncommon for a mental health

practitioner to use a diagnosis code that provides coverage and avoid one that does not.

There are several problems with the reporting of false or incomplete diagnoses: First, if a counselor lies about the diagnosis, or intentionally omits material that if known to the insurance company makes the whole condition noncovered, insurance fraud is being committed. Second, although a professional counselor may seem to be doing the patient a favor by allowing him or her to obtain insurance reimbursement, the more severe label attached to the condition may haunt the client in the future when it comes to obtaining health insurance or even in connection with obtaining a job.

Professional counselors must report all claims directly, honestly, and fairly. A claim form should accurately reflect the true diagnosis and the procedure rendered, and the client's charts and records should provide ample documentation about what occurred. The time and length of treatments should be noted accurately and should be supported by other evidence, such as scheduling calendars and treatment notes. Remember that insurance companies and regulatory agencies are likely to review bills and records. Professional counselors should practice as if they expect that someone will look over their shoulder at any moment—because someone probably will!

Charging insurance carriers for failed appointments. Another example of insurance fraud is charging a failed appointment as a psychotherapy session to an insurance carrier. It is standard practice for most counselors to charge a client for a failed appointment, but this should always be a fee issue between the client and the professional counselor and never involve the insurance carrier.

Charging lower fees for clients who do not have insurance. Insurance carriers view as fraud the practice of charging clients without insurance lower fees while charging clients with insurance a higher rate on a routine basis. Insurance companies reimburse upon usual and customary rate, perhaps as modified by their criteria. But a rate raised especially for the carrier is not usual and customary. In addition, many practitioners in the past have allowed certain clients the opportunity to pay "insurance only," thus waiving the clients' copayment. In both cases, if the professional counselor desires to discount his or her services, the discounted fee should be charged to the insurance carrier. Applicable copayments to the reduced amount will still apply. In cases where the client has no insurance, the professional counselor is advised to charge the full fee, and if the client is unable to pay this at a later date even with liberal pay arrangements, the fee should be written off in conjunction with established collection procedures for every other client in the practice.

Malpractice Issues

The subject of counseling malpractice is to be covered in Volume 12 of the ACA Legal Series. Here issues are discussed only in relation to third-party reimbursement.

Malpractice is generally defined in most states as the failure of a practitioner to treat a patient in the same manner as a reasonable, prudent practitioner of the same or similar specialty under the same circumstances. In any malpractice case, the plaintiff is required to have an expert to provide his or her case. For cases involving counselors, that expert will be another professional counselor or (in some states) a professional claiming to understand the standards of professional counseling. Such an expert will testify that the conduct of the practitioner in this particular case fell below the standard of care of the normal, prudent practitioner. Without an expert, a plaintiff cannot make a case. Similarly, a defendant needs an expert to testify that the care in question was within the standard of care of the reasonable, prudent practitioner.

As a practical matter, in most jurisdictions (with the exception of some jurisdictions, such as California, Florida, and New York), it is difficult to sustain a malpractice case over a mere error in judgment unless there are catastrophic results. Juries generally allow professionals leeway in exercising their judgment, recognizing that the practice of various professions is as much as art as a science.

In mental health, however, the existence of the *DSM-III-R* may create difficulties. Few specialties have the kind of detailed diagnostic manual that mental health professions have in *DSM-III-R*. For example, a general surgeon might investigate certain indications in trying to ascertain whether a patient has appendicitis. But in the final analysis, that often becomes a judgment call based on personal factors and a great deal of instinct. A professional counselor, however, has a list of symptoms that should enable him or her to diagnose a patient as having a major depressive illness. If the professional counselor fails to diagnose the illness, it is relatively easy for a plaintiff to confront the counselor with the *DSM-III-R* and its list of symptoms and demand to know why the counselor did not consider the diagnosis suggested by *DSM-III-R*. Nevertheless, failures to obtain the proper diagnosis are rarely catastrophic in mental health, with the obvious exception of the failure to identify a suicidal or homicidal condition. Thus many lawsuits involving mental health providers involve the failure to properly identify a suicidal or homicidal condition and take appropriate steps to protect lives.

Perhaps the greatest number of malpractice suits seen in the mental health area involve inappropriate sexual contact between a mental health care provider and a client. No credible standard allows for sexual contact between a professional counselor and a client. Having sex with a client is malpractice. If the patient choses to follow with a lawsuit, it is an automatic malpractice victory. The question is not guilt; the question is how much the damages will be.

Dual relationships—that is, situations in which professional counselors have dealings with clients that go beyond the therapist-client relationship—can also be a malpractice issue. Accepting barter (goods or services) from clients in return for counseling services is one way such dual relationships might be formed. Professional counselors should refrain from entering into any personal, financial, professional, or other relationship that may affect or impair the professional counselor's objectivity.

Another issue of concern is therapist-client privilege. In some states, the conversations between a professional counselor and a client are privileged and not subject to disclosure except by permission of the client. Some states do not recognize the privilege. Because the ethics of the profession forbid disclosure without a client's permission, irrespective of the status of state law, problems can be avoided by always seeking to keep the client's confidences safe. In the event of court action or subpoenas, consultation with legal counsel is recommended.

One common thread applies to both billing and malpractice: client satisfaction. A good provider-client relationship is the best preventative medicine to avoid malpractice suits; it is also the surest way to get paid.

 # Strategies for Maximizing Reimbursement

In efforts to secure—and maximize—third-party payments for their services, counselors need to consider the issues presented here related to filing claims, using the HCFA-1500 form, using procedure codes, insurance audits, rejected claims, errors in payment, and such other alternatives as affiliation with managed care organizations.

Filing Claims

Any professional counselor wishing to enter the third-party payment arena must realize the crucial fact that health insurance reimbursement is based upon the medical model. Thus reimbursement for services rendered is based upon the client demonstrating a bona fide medical diagnosis of an emotional or mental disorder and meeting the criteria for medical necessity as defined by the insurance carrier. In addition, services rendered must fit within the medical model and be medically necessary.

Many professional counselors have difficulty accepting the medical model. They feel that the medical model is a psychiatrically oriented system in which many counseling services do not fit. In a sense this assumption is correct: Given the strict definition, many services provided by a professional counselor, such as career counseling, educational counseling, educational testing, career assessments, and marital therapy when the problem is truly marital, are not medically necessary. Professional counselors should not expect to be reimbursed by health insurance carriers for these services.

Professional counselors must also realize that their clients are not "entitled" to third-party reimbursement. No matter how competent and ethical the therapist, some state laws or insurance regulations can and will legally deny reimbursement to clients of professional counselors. This may be difficult to accept, but professional counselors should not personalize an insurance company's rejection—which has no bearing on the counselors' professional competency or worth.

Professional counselors must further realize that they are not a part of the health insurance contract. The contract exists between the client or his or her employer and the insurance carrier. Professional counselors should not lose sight of the facts that the health insurance carrier is only a third party to an intense and professional relationship and that the primary responsibility for the payment of the services rendered is a matter between the client and the counselor. Thus at intake the professional counselor should make this known to the client and reiterate that the client remains totally responsible for the payment of fees regardless of third-party payment issues.

In an effort to establish a relationship with a client, a professional counselor is often overaccommodating in the matter of fees, and it is difficult for professional counselors who are trained to be empathic and helpful not to work as closely as possible with the client on obtaining third-party reimbursement. Therefore the professional counselor may be tempted to file an insurance claim on behalf of the client with a diagnosis or procedure that ensures third-party reimbursement even when a different diagnosis is the correct one. The professional counselor is strongly advised to render a diagnosis that is the least severe—and most accurate. Rendering a diagnosis that is inaccurate for the sake of ensuring reimbursement is both unethical and illegal. Further, the procedure code should accurately reflect the services rendered.

The professional counselor should also keep in mind that any client can become an enemy, and that insurance companies are increasingly enhancing their fraud divisions in order to identify and prosecute practitioners guilty of insurance fraud. Mental health professionals do go to jail for insurance fraud. In addition, professional counselors should be absolutely certain that the services for which they are seeking reimbursement are within the scope of their license as well as within the ethical guidelines of their respective professional state, local, and national professional organizations.

HCFA-1500 Form

The HCFA-1500 form is universally accepted by Medicare, Medicaid, CHAMPUS, and other insurance carriers. Although many private insurance carriers have their own forms, they are similar to the HCFA-1500 form, and the private carriers may in fact accept the HCFA-1500 form as the basis for reimbursement. HCFA-1500 forms and completion instructions can be obtained from regional HCFA offices (Medicare, 1992).

Procedure Codes

Professional counselors should make every effort to be aware of appropriate procedure codes for psychotherapy-related services. Professional counselors should be familiar with, if not purchase a copy of, *CPT-4* (the most recent edition of *Physicians Current Procedural Terminology*, published by the American Medical Association in 1991). Commonly used procedural codes when filing mental health claims include the following:

90801 - psychiatric diagnostic interview and examination including history, mental status, or disposition
90830 - psychological testing per hour
90831 - telephone consultation with or about patient for psychiatric, therapeutic, or diagnostic purposes.
90843 - individual psychotherapy, 20-30 minutes
90844 - individual psychotherapy, 45-50 minutes

90847 - family therapy
90853 - group therapy
90849 - multiple family group therapy
90887 - interpretation and explanation of results
90889 - preparation of report of psychiatric status
99080 - special report.

Insurance Audits

Most insurance carriers obtain permission from their subscribers to have access to their medical records. This access allows the insurance carrier to verify charges and procedures rendered. Professional counselors should realize that insurance carriers have a legal right to examine medical records and that insurance audits are occurring with ever greater frequency. Professional counselors should view the medical record as their best friend or worst enemy, based upon what is entered in the client's chart. The following records guidelines are suggested for outpatient sessions (Blue Cross/Blue Shield of Virginia, 1992, pp. 7-8):

- **Clinical Evaluation**
  A clinical evaluation is documented in the medical record and includes:

  1. the presenting problem:
     a. history of present illness
     b. evidence of personal distress
     c. impairment of functioning
  2. medical history including medication and allergies
  3. previous treatment and outcome
  4. social history
  5. family history
  6. history of alcohol and drug use
  7. mental status exam
  8. appropriate diagnosis
  9. intervention technique and rationale for selection in relation to diagnosis

10. initial treatment plan with goals of treatment, including estimated number of treatment sessions to achieve goals
11. signature and credentials of provider.

- **Psychotherapy Notes**
  Clinical notes must be documented in a timely manner and include:

  1. patient's name
  2. date of service
  3. type and length of session
  4. individuals present at the session
  5. therapeutic focus
     a. update of treatment plan after each sessions
     b. methods of treatment (e.g., pharmacotherapy, electroconvulsive therapy)
     c. progress report
     d. estimated number of treatment sessions after each of six visits
     e. type of therapy (e.g., group, individual)
  6. summary of treatment outcome upon termination
  7. signature and credentials of provider.

Rejected Claims

Insurance claims can be rejected for a variety of reasons, many of which have already been suggested. These reasons include unmet deductibles, preexisting conditions, nonreimbursable services, unapproved providers, previously met limits for mental health coverage, policies not being in effect when the service was rendered, nonreimbursable diagnoses, or incorrect or incomplete insurance claim forms.

Often error on the part of claims processors is to blame for the rejection. In these cases, claims processors—who are often overworked and unaware of mental health issues—may misread, misenter, or misinterpret the claim before them. When processing errors occur, the professional counselor should send a letter or compose a form letter for such situations. Included in this letter should be the subscriber's identification number, the group number, the claim number, a copy of the rejected claim, and the reason why the professional counselor feels that an error has occurred.

Rejected claims are often frustrating for the professional counselor and his or her client. It may be difficult not to see the rejected claim as a rejection of personal competence or as a conscious lack of respect on the part of the insurance carrier. It can also be embarrassing in terms of status lost with the client. The professional counselor must keep a rational mind and approach this situation objectively:

- When the reason for the rejection is not clear, write the company and request the exact reason why the claim was rejected. The letter should be professionally written, polite, and to the point. Avoid any threatening or belligerent tones. Once you have ascertained the reason for the rejection, request that the claim be reconsidered and provide any additional clarification requested by the insurance carrier.
- If the claim is still rejected, and the rejection is based on issues related to noncoverage of services rendered by professional counselors, the client or the client's employer may wish to apply pressure upon the insurance carrier to honor the claim. In certain circumstances the client, not the counselor, has the right to seek legal action against the insurance carrier for a rejected claim. The professional counselor may want to contact the American Counseling Association (ACA) or other state or national professional organizations that may be able to render additional assistance in educating the insurance carrier as to the role of professional counselors and affecting payment.

Nahl (1992) suggested that the following information be submitted to the insurance company if a claim is denied because of a policy not to reimburse for the services of professional counselors:

1. copy of state law regarding freedom of choice statutes if applicable
2. sections of the state regulations regarding the regulations of professional counselors

3. copy of any national certifications (e.g., CCMHC, AAMFT)
4. curriculum vita
5. contested claim
6. polite and positive cover letter expressing hope that the company will honor their policyholder's choice of service providers and not discriminate against a competent licensed psychotherapist.

Errors in Payment

Errors often occur. The insurance carrier can either under- or overpay a claim. If an overpayment has been made by a non-insurance carrier, the professional counselor should notify the insurance carrier and refund the excess amount voluntarily. If an overpayment has been made and the professional counselor is made aware of such, it is best to repay the overpaid amount as soon as possible. If there is an underpayment, the professional counselor should again write a professional, polite letter to the insurance carrier stating the reasons why he or she feels that an underpayment has been made and requesting reconsideration of the claim.

In certain circumstances, even with the assignment of benefits endorsed to the professional counselor by the client, the client, rather than the professional counselor, may receive the insurance carrier's check. The professional counselor is advised to attempt to collect this amount from the client. If the client refuses, the professional counselor should contact the insurance carrier, which may reprocess the claim and attempt to obtain a refund from the subscriber. In many cases, however, the professional counselor may have no other recourse than to attempt to collect the funds from the client.

Other Alternatives

Professional counselors should also explore affiliation with organizations such as managed care companies, employee assistance programs (EAPs), health maintenance organizations (HMOs), and preferred provider organizations (PPOs). Such affiliations can enhance referral tracks essential for the professional counselor in private practice. Although belonging to such organizations usually means providing services at a discounted fee, the competition to participate can be keen, given the overall trend toward managed care and negotiated discounted fees.

Estimates vary, but there is little disagreement that most Americans will be under some form of managed care as the year 2000 approaches. Herrington (1990) reported that 40% of Americans were already covered by some kind of managed care plan, 20% in HMOs and another 20% in PPOs.

As more attention is paid to health care costs by employers, insurance carriers, and federal and state governments, the trend toward distinct decreases in traditional insurance plans will certainly continue. Professional counselors should be vigilant to overall health care trends and react accordingly. Given the proliferation of managed care, PPOs, and HMOs, the harsh reality is that many practitioners will be working more hours for fewer dollars.

As professional counselors consider whether to participate in certain managed or other alternative plans, they should carefully investigate and consider the track record of the managed care organization in question. Is the organization really interested in quality of care or just in saving money? How does case management occur? What services are covered/excluded? How are clients referred? How are providers compensated? What are the discounted rates? What diagnoses are excluded? Can a provider appeal a denial and how? What are the terms of the contract? How much is the client financially penalized for seeking services outside the organization?

Affiliation with a PPO, HMO, or managed care organization can open windows of opportunity for professional counselors in areas from which they may be excluded by traditional insurance contracts. This may happen as various organizations allow for payment to professional counselors as part of their national policy. Conversely, certain organizations may exclude professional counselors on a national basis, and thus professional counselors in states with mandated benefits may not be reimbursed by certain managed care organizations without benefit of extraterritoriality laws.

Helping Clients Understand the Reimbursement Process

Many clients seeking the services of professional counselors are either naive or misinformed as to the insurance reimbursement process. Many come with a sense of entitlement or expectation that services will or should be paid in full. Additionally, clients often are not informed as to the fact that most reimbursement for mental health services involves a copayment on their behalf. Clients often assume that they are entitled to reimbursement for mental health services, and although morally they may be correct, this is often not the case. Professional counselors should be sensitive to the misconceptions of clients regarding health care reimbursement and not assume that every client has a full and working knowledge of the health insurance claim process. The professional counselor should consider the following points in helping the client to understand the reimbursement process:

- The issue of fees is an issue between counselor and client. Simply put, the counselor renders the services, and the client is responsible to the counselor for payment of that service. If the client possesses a health insurance contract that includes coverage for mental health services, that contract is an additional resource that the client has in his or her possession to assist the client in paying for services rendered by the counselor.

- The client should be informed as to the differences among a professional counselor, social worker, psychiatrist, and psychologist. Often a client will enter counseling assuming that the term *psychologist* is generic and that a professional counselor will be reimbursed, although this may not be the case.
- Clients often do not understand concepts of deductibles, usual, customary, and reasonable (UCR) rates, copayments, and contract limitations (caps). Professional counselors should be prepared to explain these concepts patiently when asked.
- The client should be aware that when filing for third-party reimbursement, the insurance carrier will at least be provided a diagnostic code and in some cases will be privy to confidential information.
- In cases of managed care, the client should be informed that a fourth party (case manager) will be reviewing the case, be approving continued treatment and insurance reimbursement, and be privy to confidential information.
- Clients should be assisted in understanding that certain procedures rendered by professional counselors are not directly related to a medical necessity or medical treatment. Thus, for example, career counseling, educational testing, and counseling for such problems as marital dysfunctioning or occupational dissatisfaction most probably will not be reimbursed.
- Clients should understand that professional counselors must ethically and responsibly file insurance claims reflecting the most accurate and least restrictive diagnosis and procedure code. Professional counselors can not and should not alter a diagnosis code or procedure merely to assist the client in achieving reimbursement.

Frequently Asked Questions

Q. What are mandated benefits, and how do they help the professional counselor?

A. The term *mandated benefits* refers to specific services for which state law requires insurance companies to reimburse clients or providers. The term is used in two different ways: First, state law may mandate that certain types of health care be provided in all insurance policies. For example, many states require that insurance companies pay for a certain amount of prenatal care, for certain types of treatment for substance abuse, and for certain types of mental health care. Were these services not mandated, insurance companies would not be required to provide them to their subscribers, and probably would not do so. States have, however, determined that some of these services are so important that providing them should be a condition of allowing an insurance company to sell policies in the state.

Second, the term *mandated benefits* refers to the freedom of the subscriber to choose which kind of practitioner will provide a certain type of care. For example, a mandated-benefit statute might say that in any instance a policy provides for psychiatric care by a psychiatrist or psychologist, the insurance company should reimburse the subscriber for the same services when

provided by a licensed professional counselor or social worker.
Because many insurance companies historically have excluded
reimbursement to health care providers who are not medical
doctors, this type of freedom-of-choice legislation is important,
both to consumers and professional counselors.

**Q. What are "bare-bones" policies—now being issued by
some insurance companies?**

A. Insurance companies, particularly the various Blue Shield
companies, assert that mandated-benefit laws render basic
health care policies prohibitively expensive for many people.
The insurance companies argue that the requirement that
they pay for mandated benefits is a major cause of the large
uninsured population in this country. As a result, in many
states, insurance companies are lobbying to abolish mandated-
benefit laws, or to allow, under certain circumstances, the sale
of bare-bones policies, which do not have mandated-benefit
provisions. Many of these bare-bones policies exclude mental
health care.

**Q. Can a practitioner legally bill a carrier for a phantom
visit in order to help a patient reduce the balance owed
the practitioner when the services, in fact, were rendered at some other time but not billed to the insurance
company?**

A. No. Many insurance companies have a limit on the number
of weekly sessions they will reimburse, or on the length of these
sessions. In these circumstances, it is illegal for the practitioner
to bill for phantom visits that did not occur during a time, for
example, a vacation, when services were not rendered. In other
words, if the client goes on a 2-week vacation, the practitioner
cannot submit bills for visits during this period to make up for
uncompensated visits from an earlier time. This practice is
deemed to be fraud.

All billing must be truthful and honest, representing in an
accurate way when the services were rendered, the length of the
services, and the health care provider. Any misrepresentation,
whether by omission or commission, deprives the insurance

company of the right to contest paying for the service based on what actually occurred.

Q. If a client has two independent diseases, one of which is a covered disease and one of which is not, can the covered disease be reported to the insurance company and the noncovered disease not be reported?

A. Generally, no. Again, the guiding standard is that information provided to the insurance company must be honest and truthful and neither by omission or commission misrepresent the true status of the client. The difficulty is that sometimes diseases are truly independent, and sometimes they are not. For example, many policies will not cover treatment for marital stress but will cover treatment for panic disorder. Though panic disorder might be caused by marital distress, it is an independent illness. Although it is arguable that panic disorder arising from marital problems is a separate, independent disease, the better practice is to report the whole context of the mental health problem rather than to assert that the patient has panic disorder unconnected to a noncovered illness.

Q. What is malpractice?

A. Malpractice is the failure of a health care practitioner to act in a professional situation in the same manner as a reasonable, prudent practitioner of a similar specialty. The way in which a reasonable, prudent practitioner deals with a client in a set of circumstances is called the *standard of care*. Violating the standard of care means that the practitioner charged with malpractice has not acted in the same way that a reasonable and prudent colleague would under the same, or similar, circumstances. Many malpractice claims have surfaced when clinicians alter their clinical work or make special provisions in order to "play the third-party game" in order to maximize insurance reimbursement.

The lion's share of malpractice cases for health care providers concerns the failure to diagnose and manage suicidal or homicidal patients. This is an area in which great care should be taken, given the obviously disastrous potential consequences of misdiagnosis or mistreatment. An additional area in which malpractice cases occur involves inappropriate sexual or social contact between a health care provider and a client. These relationships tend to be malpractice per se, that is, automatically malpractice, and obviously should be avoided.

Q. What is the best diagnosis to insure insurance reimbursement?

A. The best diagnosis is the one that is most consistent with the client's clinical presentation. The issue of whether or not insurance reimbursement will occur should not in any way affect the clinical judgment of the clinician.

Q. Why do some insurance carriers pay for the services of professional counselors in some circumstances and not in others?

A. It is important to remember that insurance carriers have different contracts with different employers. In some cases a certain insurance carrier may be required by law to reimburse for the services of professional counselors in a given state. However, that same insurance carrier may be administering a self-insured plan for an employer in the same state. As such, the insurance carrier is not obligated to pay for the services of professional counselors because a self-insured plan is exempt from state law.

Often cases may involve the concept of extraterritoriality. In such situations, a given insurance carrier may be obligated to pay for the services provided in a given state as part of a contract written in that state, but that same insurance carrier may not be obligated to pay if the contract with the employer is written with a company based out of state, even though employees are in the state in which the insurance mandate occurs.

Guidelines for Practice

When you enter the third-party arena. . .

1. Be as knowledgeable of health insurance issues as possible.
2. Learn the legislative statutes in the state in which you practice.
3. Familiarize yourself with diagnostic codes (*DSM-III-R*), procedural codes (*CPT-4*), and insurance carrier policies and regulations.
4. Accept the fact that health insurance reimbursement is based upon a medical model.
5. Accept the reality that from time to time insurance carriers have yet to learn the scope of practice for professional counselors.

When you file insurance claims. . .

1. Always keep adequate documentation of services rendered.
2. File insurance claim forms properly and completely.
3. Provide the most accurate, least restrictive diagnosis possible, regardless of whether the diagnostic code is reimbursable.
4. State the exact nature of services rendered, regardless of whether the procedure is reimbursable.
5. File claim forms in a timely manner.

6. Follow established guidelines in appealing rejected claims. If still rejected, follow guidelines outlined in the Strategies for Maximizing Reimbursement chapter.

If you want to prevent legal problems. . .

1. Avoid discounts and other financial arrangements to clients that may violate insurance regulations and thus be construed as insurance fraud, such as accepting "insurance only" as payment for services and waiving the client's copayment.
2. Do not provide services that are not within the scope of practice for professional counselors in the state in which you practice.
3. Do not accept barter (accepting goods or services from clients) in return for counseling services.
4. Do not charge lower fees for clients who do not have insurance while charging clients who carry insurance a higher rate on a routine basis.
5. Do not charge a missed appointment as a psychotherapy session to an insurance carrier.
6. Avoid the temptation to stretch a diagnosis or provide a very broad and general diagnosis solely for the purpose of achieving third-party reimbursement.
7. Always place the name of the person actually providing the service on the claim form. Do not fall into the trap of filing an insurance claim under a supervisor's license without being honest as to who actually delivered the service.
8. Do not misstate procedures rendered.

When you deal with third-party reimbursers, remember. . .

1. Many insurance carriers remain naive as to the qualifications and scope of practice of professional counselors.
2. Do not personalize rejections. Most claim rejections are not a reflection on the competence or qualifications of professional counselors but rather a reflection of longstanding, more traditional policies and procedures.
3. The insurance industry is constantly under change. Regulations, state statutes, and renewal contracts all can change dramatically the nature of any client's insurance coverage.

4. Never feel entitled to insurance reimbursement. The contract for insurance reimbursements exists between the insurance carrier and the client or the client's employer, not the provider.
5. Be vigilant and keep abreast of overall trends within the third-party reimbursement area as well as specific legislative and regulatory changes as they occur.

 # Summary

Third-party reimbursement for the services of professional counselors continues to be an issue that varies from state to state. In some states, professional counselors are gaining in their ability to obtain third-party reimbursement. In other states, professional counselors have seen a decline in their ability to gain reimbursement, and in some states little movement in any direction has been noted. With the influx of managed care, there is the possibility of a fourth party to the counseling process (first party is client, second party is therapist, third party is insurance reimburser, and fourth party is managed care). All of this implies a dynamic process for which there is no definitive advice that applies to all professional counselors nationwide. In addition, while professional counselors attempt to gain inclusion in the world of third-party reimbursement, the national trend is to cut reimbursement for all mental health services. What impact the national political process will have on the possible implementation of a national health program further obscures the picture as it relates to the future.

In the interim, professional counselors should continue to hone their clinical skills, work toward the establishment of a professional and ethical practice, and educate themselves as much as possible to the issue of third-party reimbursement for mental health services.

This monograph attempts to discuss as globally as possible the issues of third-party reimbursement for professional counselors. It is designed to sensitize the reader to the issues involved and to provide guidelines as appropriate. Nevertheless, professional counselors should consult with their private attorneys, state professional organizations, insurance carriers, and employers in the areas in which they work to gain more specific interpretations of the third-party reimbursement issues in relation to their particular scope of practice in the area in which they practice.

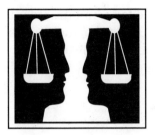

Discussion Questions

1. Discuss the concept of *participating provider*. What implications does this concept have for the professional counselor in terms of rates of reimbursement and obligations to the insurance carrier?

2. Discuss the concept of *freedom of choice* and how it affects insurance reimbursement related to professional counselors.

3. Discuss exclusions to state insurance mandates, including the implications of ERISA, extraterritoriality, and federally funded health reimbursement programs.

4. How should a professional counselor proceed when a request for insurance reimbursement is denied?

5. Discuss ways in which mental health clinicians can be guilty of insurance fraud in the process of filing insurance claims.

6. Discuss the supervisory arrangements necessary in order to be eligible to participate in treating Medicare clients.

7. Discuss the implications of the varying state requirements for the licensing of professional counselors. What are the impli-

cations in terms of national recognition of professional counselors for third-party reimbursement?

8. What are the implications of managed care as it pertains to
third-party reimbursement for professional counselors and
the conduct of clinical practice?

9. Many professional counselors are eligible for reimbursement
by CHAMPUS. Certain requirements must be met to be
eligible and protocols followed. Please discuss these issues.

Suggested Readings

Covin, T. M. (1990). *How to collect third-party payments. The professional counselor's guide to successful third-party reimbursement.* Ozark, AL: Center for Counseling and Development. A comprehensive manual that provides historical as well as general information related to the reimbursement of professional counselors. In addition, this publication provides nuts-and-bolts advice and guidelines for filing insurance claims.

Psychotherapy Finances, 1016 Clemons St., Jupiter, FL 33477. Monthly publication that outlines overall trends in the insurance and managed care industry in addition to regular discussions of private practice issues.

Small, R. F. (1991). *Maximizing third-party reimbursement in your mental health practice.* Sarasota, FL: Professional Resource Exchange. Explains key concepts vital to an awareness of the area of third-party reimbursement for mental health services. Also provides concrete data in order to maximize third-party reimbursement potential.

References

American Medical Association. (1991). *Physicians current procedural terminology—CPT-4* (4th ed.). Chicago, IL: Author.

American Psychiatric Association (1987). *Diagnostic and statistical manual of mental disorders,* (3rd ed., rev.). *(DSM-III-R).* Washington, DC: Author.

Blue Cross/Blue Shield Association. (1992). *Washington report.* Washington, DC: Author.

Blue Cross/Blue Shield of Virginia. (1992). *Outpatient guidelines.* Richmond, VA: Author.

Covin, T. M. (1990a). *How to collect third-party payments. The professional counselor's guide to successful third-party reimbursement.* Ozark, AL: Center for Counseling and Development.

Covin, T. M. (1990b). Freedom of choice and the federal employees health benefits plan. *The Advocate, 13*(5), 5.

Covin, T. M. (1992, January). Freedom of choice and uniform standards for MHCs. *The Advocate,* 3.

Fee and practice survey report. (1992). *Psychotherapy Finances, 14*(12), 1-8.

Herrington, B.S. (1990). Pros, cons of managed care aired in annual meeting debate. *Psychiatric News,* pp. 4, 24.

Kovacs, A. (1988). The changing force of insurance reimbursement. *Georgia Psychologist, 41*(1), 21-26.

Koyanagi, Z. (1988). *Operating help: A mental health advocate's guide to Medicaid.* Alexandria, VA: National Mental Health Association.

Medicare. (1992). *HCFA-1500 claim form completion instructions. Information on Medicare.* Richmond, VA: The Travelers.

Nahl, M. (1992). Reimbursement issues: How to appeal a denial by an insurer. *Headlines,* 5(1), 5.

Office of Civilian Health and Medical Program of the Uniformed Services. (1988). *CHAMPUS provider handbook.* Aurora, CO: Author.

Pennsylvania Blue Shield. (1989). *Blue Shield reference guide.* Camp Hill: PA: Author.

Small, R. F. (1991). *Maximizing third-party reimbursement in your mental health practice.* Sarasota, FL: Professional Resource Exchange.

Stromberg, Z. D., Haggarty, D. J., Leibenleft, R. F., McMillan, M. H., et al. (1988). *The psychologist's legal handbook.* Washington, DC: The Council for the National Registry of Health Service Providers in Psychology.

U.S. Department of Health and Human Services, Health Care Financing Administration. (1990, August). *Medicare manual, part III.* Washington, DC: Author.

Whiting, L. (1989). *State comparisons of laws regulating social work.* Silver Springs, MD: National Association of Social Workers.